Putting Values into Practice

Building your approach and pedagogy for playing and learning outdoors

Jan White and Liz Edwards

The Natural Play Principles have been developed by
Jan White in partnership with Suzanne Scott,
Ann Thompson and Menna Godfrey
(© 2011, revised 2018)

Professor Jan White is co-founder and strategic director of Early Childhood Outdoors. She is author of the Core Values for Outdoor Play and editor of Outdoor Provision in the Early Years (Sage 2011).

Liz Edwards is founder and chief imaginer of Muddy Faces. She is author of Knife Use with Groups - a Forest School Leaders Guide and creator of the Outdoor Hub.

Copyright

Putting Values into Practice concept, text and images © Jan White and Liz Edwards (2019)

The text of the Natural Play Principles are © Jan White, Suzanne Scott, Ann Thompson and Menna Godfrey (2011, revised 2018); remaining text © Jan White (2019)

Cover image by Carol Duffy

Photographs © Carol Duffy, © Liz Edwards, © Menna Godfrey, © Ann Thompson, © Jan White

Acknowledgements

Many thanks to the children, adults and settings who have so generously contributed images for this booklet, including Ann Thompson, Carol Duffy & the Duffy family, Claire Foster & Windsor Centre for Children and Families, Menna Godfrey & Quackers, Liz Edwards & the Edwards family and friends, Suzanne Scott & Sandfield Natural Play Centre.

Disclaimer

The contents of this publication have been provided to help increase the understanding and confidence of practitioners aiming to develop outdoor play with young children. As with any aspect of early years provision, it is always necessary to carry out ongoing benefit-risk assessment and management according to the specific children, situation and conditions pertaining.

The author, publisher and contributors cannot take any responsibility for the use of the guidance and ideas given, and cannot accept any legal responsibility or liability for any harm arising from the use of the guidance, resources and experiences presented in this publication.

Contents

1   The Opening Up The Outdoors initiative

3   Moving from values towards practice

Guiding principles:
- 5   A natural curriculum
- 7   The natural world
- 9   Authentic experiences
- 11   Embodied learning
- 13   Imagination, creativity and science
- 15   Child-paced learning
- 17   Adventure and adventuring
- 19   Risk is an intelligent behaviour
- 21   Belonging and caring
- 23   Building an ecological identity
- 25   Parental engagement and involvement
- 27   Enabling adults to enable children

29   Gateways to natural play

Much has happened over the past decade in progressing the right of all young children to access play, and the learning that takes place through their play, in the outdoors. We now have a broad consensus across the UK and at all levels from Government to practitioners and parents, that outdoor play matters and that **'outdoor learning'** is important – and increasingly, that this is as significant as indoor learning.

Along the way, many settings have been exploring their approach to outdoor play and learning, and several are pushing at the boundaries of what it really means to be in the outdoors, what kind of outdoor environment can be harnessed, such as woodlands, beaches and the street, and in what ways the outdoors can be used for the benefit of young children. Exciting times are ahead for the field of outdoor play and learning!

However, many early years settings still have to work with difficult access to the outdoors, uninspiring outdoor spaces, restricted funds for design, resources, training, outdoor clothing and so on, staff who are early on in their own journey of working well with the outdoor environment, and parents who are not yet fully on board with the setting's intentions for learning outdoors. There is still much work to do! The outdoors has so much potential to offer to young children: **how can we unlock and open up this fabulous treasure trove?**

Opening Up The Outdoors builds on the remarkable success of Jan White and Liz Edwards' previous Mud Play initiative, which aimed to deepen the understanding, importance, value and range of experiences from mud play as continuous provision and to support practitioners to achieve this (Making a Mud Kitchen 2011). This larger initiative shares the vision and goal of *more children thriving outdoors, more often and for longer, benefiting from richer and more meaningful environments offering authentic, rewarding and satisfying experiences* through a long term, three cornered approach tackling the **WHY**, **WHAT** and **HOW** of really good outdoor play.

Establishing beliefs

The **'establishing beliefs'** booklets underpin understanding and thinking about being outdoors in the early years – providing firm foundations for moving forwards. As well as providing this value base, the **Opening Up the Outdoors** initiative includes two 'how to do it' strands that will help practitioners to provide learning through play outdoors that is rich, effective and satisfying – **WHAT** needs to be worked upon to fully harness the potential of the outdoors, and **HOW** to create the rich experiences that make for really good outdoor play.

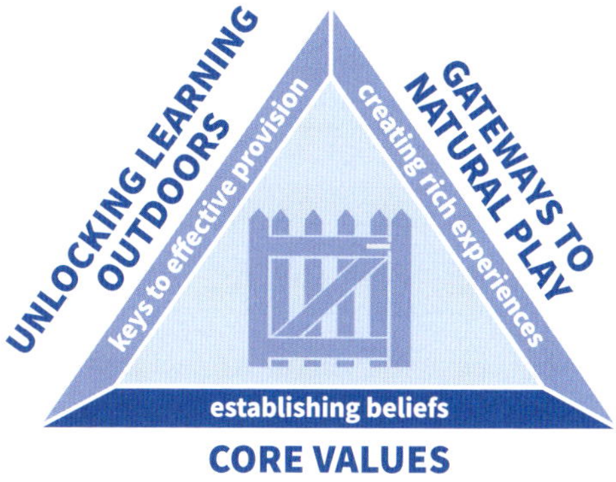

Moving from values towards practice

Building your approach and pedagogy for playing and learning outdoors

As the first and crucial step of addressing the **WHY** of outdoor play in the Opening Up the Outdoors initiative, the booklet **Valuing the Outdoors** (Muddy Faces 2018) presented ten core values (developed in 2004 by the Vision and Values Partnership) which describe the **underpinning beliefs** held across the UK about high quality outdoor experience for young children. These values create a firm basis for all thinking about playing and learning outdoors, providing solid foundations from which all decisions about provision and practice for young children should be made. However, values are large and nebulous: some further stages are necessary in order for us to be able to turn this value base into actual practice.

Whilst 'values' articulate internally held general beliefs, turning them into 'principles' provides a more concrete set of aims giving more specific **external 'rules' for enacting our internal values** in the real world.

From this set of guiding principles we can construct our approach to teaching and learning – our philosophy and 'pedagogy', or, how we actually **want to behave and intend to act** with and for young children outdoors.

The final stage in the process is to work from this clear pedagogical base (our philosophy and approach) to determine **what we actually do in practice** – the very many decisions and actions we carry out through provision and adult support in order to enact our values and desired pedagogical approach.

Working from the core values for outdoor play and learning in the early years, this second foundation **Opening Up the Outdoors** booklet presents a set of **twelve guiding principles** that can guide the development of your approach, provision, pedagogy and practice towards achieving the vision for all young children. Together, these principles articulate a child-centred and nature-focused approach called **Natural Play** (White et al. 2011 & 2018).

Developed over many years as a working collaboration between Jan White (Early Childhood Natural Play), Suzanne Scott (Sandfield Natural Play Centre), Ann Thompson (Naturally Creative and Sandfield Natural Play Centre) and Menna Godfrey (Quackers Playgroup & Natural Play Centre), **Natural Play** foregrounds both the child's inner and emerging **natural curriculum** and the very significant role of the **natural world** in enabling this. *Natural Play enables children's natural ways of growing, learning and thriving with the help of the natural world.*

The Natural Play Principles are lived out every day through the intentions and actions in leadership, curriculum, provision and practice at Sandfield and Quackers; so they are presented here as what 'we' believe and seek to do all the time, for every child and family and every member of the team.

Through making a child-centred philosophy and nature-focused approach explicit, with a set of **'Natural Play Principles'** providing the rules for enacting core values about outdoor play and learning, this booklet aims to support the process of turning the underpinning beliefs and values expressed in **Valuing the Outdoors** into meaningful actions for practice. Therefore after setting out each Natural Play Principle, we offer some ways to start putting this guiding principle into practice. These actions are components of the 'keys to effective provision' in **Unlocking Learning Outdoors** - the **WHAT** of the Opening Up the Outdoors initiative.

A natural Curriculum

At the heart of our thinking is a belief that children's own need and drive to learn can be trusted. The young child's body and mind has its own developmental agenda and processes, which they should be empowered to find and follow. We respect their natural urge to play and enable a truly inclusive and child-led curriculum.

Putting this guiding principle into practice

Build the conviction of every adult in your setting that **children are innately curious and driven learners:** they need to find out about their world and make their own sense of it, and they will do this whenever they can!

Build belief that **what matters is what is inside each individual child**, and how we can help its expression through encouraging their own fascinations and drives. The most satisfying and deepest learning occurs through **self-driven and self-directed exploration and play,** with the careful support of tuned-in adults.

With the collaboration of your children and their families, create your own homemade mud kitchen (read Jan White and Liz Edwards' booklet **Making a Mud Kitchen** (2nd edn. Muddy Faces 2019). Document and display some of the many wonderful examples of individual drives and ways of **exploring, experimenting, theory building and meaning-making** that you see taking place.

The natural world

We believe that children need the natural world and that it looks after them. They are biologically designed to be outdoors in a nature-rich environment and therefore thrive by having everyday intimate contact with it. It provides the most generous and powerful learning environment, with great affordance for child-led learning and development.

Putting this guiding principle into practice

Focus upon the **inborn relationship** between young children and living and physical natural world (known as biophilia), working to maintain and deepen it through **lots of daily physical and playful contact** throughout the year.

Enrich your outdoor environment in any way you can with natural elements, such as sticks, stones, shells, water, sand, soil, plants, trees, natural materials, gardening, minibeasts, birds, rain, wind and sun. Start small and aim to increase the range, amount and scale over time. Make use of visits in your **locality to add to this** as much as possible.

Spend time observing just **how much natural elements provide** for children's wellbeing, learning and development – and realising how **investigative, imaginative and inventive** young children are when playing with these materials.

Use Jan White's book **Playing and Learning Outdoors** (3rd edn. Routledge 2019) as a source book to **guide and support** these developments.

Authentic experiences

Young children must have real, direct, hands-on opportunities that are experiential, meaningful and worthwhile to them. Natural Play focuses on what matters to the children - what their big ideas are and what they want to know about and do - and enables these enquires to emerge over time. It focuses on ideas and theory-making (how do things work), through daily experiences such as playing, growing, cooking and eating, woodwork, taking things apart, caring for the setting's environment and interacting with each other and nature.

Putting this guiding principle into practice

Work towards organising the materials and resources outdoors as continuous provision, so that children can **select what they need and choose what they do,** following their own drives and interests.

Focus on providing **real-life contexts and real materials** that give children access to meaningful experiences from both the human world and the physical and natural world.

When thinking about what and how to provide experiences outdoors, emphasise **direct, hands-on, experiential learning** involving use of the whole body.

Plan with the intention that children are able to **return to their enquiries and fascinations over long stretches of time** (within each day and over longer periods), so that they can continue to work on them, building and refining their ideas or theories.

Embodied learning

Central to Natural Play is the importance of physicality, movement and doing. Young children have an essential need for sensory stimulation (including motion and action) and this is best found in the natural outdoor environment. We provide a multi-sensory and movement-rich environment and curriculum for children which harnesses the therapeutic nature of being outdoors throughout the year. Appropriate clothing enables children to fully embrace whole-bodied learning.

Putting this guiding principle into practice

Work to create an outdoor environment that **encourages physicality and the simultaneous use of all external and internal senses,** especially moving in all directions and demanding use of the whole body.

Focus on learning experiences that involve **action, doing and causing effects,** and which **can be repeated over time** to build up intuitive, embodied understandings.

Make good use of the **special freedoms and feelings** of being outside, ensuring that clothing enables **whole-bodied responses**.

Read Jan White's book **Every Child a Mover** (Early Education 2015) to learn about the **central role of movement and sensory** stimulation and integration in children's health, wellbeing, development and learning. Emphasise this throughout **thinking about, planning for and interacting with** children's play outdoors.

Imagination, creativity and science

Imagination, creativity and science are at the heart of children's natural play. The drive to work things out and imagine what might be is part of being human and a major purpose of childhood. We see children as scientists, engineers, architects, artists, innovators, creators and collaborators, with feelings and thinking inextricably woven together. Natural Play seeks to feed children's curiosity, fascination, awe and deep drive to learn and make meaning. A deep understanding of schematic behaviour and theory building enables adults to support these processes.

Putting this guiding principle into practice

Make your outdoor environment **rich in real and natural materials:** sand, soil, stone, water, natural materials and plants especially.

Supply resources and tools that enable your children to **interact in many ways** with these materials, such as wheelbarrows, buckets, crates, brushes, ropes, tarpaulins and kitchen utensils.

Give children permission to move and mix materials and to use them inventively however they are inspired to. Ensure that their clothing also provides the freedom to do this.

Learn about **schema theory** and start to notice individual children's **threads of thinking**. Recognise also children's levels of **wellbeing and involvement** during such activity.

Child-paced learning

We understand that everything children take note of and want to do has value and is valuable to them. Young children must have ample time to explore, discover, create and experiment. They also need plentiful opportunities to repeat, revisit and play with their ideas. We are working with the notion of 'slowliness', attending to the detail and richness in everything children do. Therefore, we value long, unhurried periods of time together outdoors that allow children to become deeply absorbed in their play.

Putting this guiding principle into practice

Work towards giving children the daily opportunity to **be outside for as long as they choose**, with all aspects of the curriculum available in ways that capture what is special about the outdoors.

Ensure that children have stretches of **unstructured and uninterrupted time** outside so that deep enquiry has time to develop and complex play can emerge.

Emphasise the role of adults as **observers, listeners and thinkers** so that you become increasingly able to see much more of what the children are really doing and thinking about.

Place value upon times when children appear to be doing 'nothing' and pay attention to the opportunity for **downtime and reverie** in your outdoor environment.

Consider what **'next steps' should really mean** in your planning process for your children.

Adventure and adventuring

We want children and adults to be able to find excitement and a sense of wonder as they explore the world. By venturing into unknown, but secure enough, places in both real and imaginary worlds they discover new things about themselves and their world. The natural world offers a strong environment for being adventurous.

Putting this guiding principle into practice

For a young child to be adventurous, they need a background of **feeling secure, safe and sufficiently supported**. Deploy comfortable and well-placed seating so that children can quickly check in to locate adults who show that they are attentive and taking pleasure in what the child is doing.

Ample time outside every day allows the outdoor environment to become **familiar and predictable**, in turn enabling the child to venture into unfamiliar situations and enjoy the excitement of novel experiences. This security also frees the mind for **imagination and creativity**.

Work to create a **complex, nature-filled environment** that provides much that is novel or intriguing and pushes the boundaries of experience in ways that are valuable to each child.

Adventuring also needs adults who genuinely share feelings of **curiosity, fascination and pleasure** in finding things out.

Risk is an intelligent behaviour

Meaningful education requires emotional, social, physical and cognitive challenge, through which children develop confidence, competence and agency. We provide freedom, flexibility and rich experiences within a dynamic benefit/risk framework. We want children to become resilient and risk competent and to develop a 'growth mindset' that enables them to a have a go, try again and know that 'I can do it'. For this to happen, the adults supporting them must also be capable and confident working in this environment.

Putting this guiding principle into practice

Consider the **value of children challenging themselves** and that risk is not only physical. Work to **reframe attitudes to risk** so that becoming 'risk literate' is understood as valuable for developing positive dispositions and vital life skills.

Rather than using risk assessment that **removes or reduces** experiences, move towards a balanced benefit-risk management approach to **enable outdoor experiences that are valuable** for young children's learning and development.

For this to happen successfully, all supporting **adults must develop their own ability** to recognise hazards and risks, know how to manage these to make children's experiences sufficiently safe and be able to manage harmful situations when they arise.

Leaders must also constantly ensure that everyone in the team feels **positive, supported and confident** about managing challenge and risk in your outdoor provision.

Belonging and caring

Of great importance in Natural Play is a focus on wellbeing and togetherness. When children feel at home and are recognised in the group they are able to trust, be affectionate, express thoughts and feelings, and rely on others, developing a strong sense of security, belonging and support. Building from this bedrock, we foster internalised dispositions of caring, compassion and generosity towards all others. Attention to the passing of time, traces of previous use and the making of memories contribute to a sense of heritage. From the inner child outwards, we build the foundations of care and respect for ourselves, society and the planet.

Putting this guiding principle into practice

Rather than being like a playground, focus upon making your outdoor environment feel homely, with plenty of possibility for nurturing feelings of **togetherness, affection and being part of a family,** between each other and with adults.

Direct effort to consistently showing **respect to and trust in children** in small actions – these will add up over time. Trust children to help with the real tasks of caring for the outdoor environment and resources wherever possible, building this into your planning.

Demonstrate and model **looking after, caring and compassion** in lots of ways. Notice and recognise children engaging in these actions whenever and however it happens.

Involve children in creating the outdoor environment itself, for example through planting or by weaving into fences. Seeing **traces of others and leaving memories** of themselves nurtures roots and belonging.

Building an ecological identity

At the core of Natural Play is the desire to cultivate deep identification with nature as part of each child's growing sense of self. We want the child to know that they are part of nature and it is part of them, feeling no sense of separation from it. We take the view that nature's responsiveness to the play drives of the child builds the attachment to nature that in turn creates an 'ecological identity'. Extensive interactions with a nature-rich outdoor environment and building relationships with locality and community cultivate the roots of a sense of place – being at home in the outdoors. Participating in the living and physical world nourishes wonder and joy in being alive in the world, growing the appreciation, gratitude and optimism that underpin happiness, meaning and purpose throughout life.

Putting this guiding principle into practice

Work long-term to add all kinds of natural elements to your outdoor offer with emphasis on **physical contact and interaction**. Attend especially to the **sensations and feelings** that being in and with nature generates.

Make sure children can spend **lots of time immersed** in the physical and living natural world, including all types of weather.

Look for opportunities where nature can provide for children's **natural play drives** – hiding in bushes, being up high in trees or on hills, travelling along pathways, foraging and gathering sticks, shells or blackberries, transforming soil and water into muddy mixtures.

Plan for lots of **unhurried, small group visits** to the shops, streets and green spaces local to your setting.

Nourish **awe, wonder, appreciation and gratitude** for small things and everyday events. **Simple shared rituals,** such as filling wild bird feeders, can be very effective for this.

Parental engagement and involvement

Parents and carers who are fully engaged with the Natural Play principles understand and appreciate the special nature of being outdoors for their child. We share the outdoor learning of the children with their families at every opportunity and in multiple ways. By inviting parents to share our experiences outdoors throughout the year, we encourage families to take the opportunity to explore their own outdoor spaces.

Putting this guiding principle into practice

Invite parents and carers to **drop off and collect their child** in the outside area so that they often see your provision and practice in action.

Try out several ways to help parents/carers be aware and **appreciate how their child feels when playing outdoors** – and the richness of what they are learning and how they are developing through this play. Find out which method works for each family.

Hold regular open sessions where parents and carers can engage in **practical workshops outside**, such as den making and mud kitchen play, allowing them to experience the feelings of this kind of play for themselves.

Provide **ideas and information** to help families to enjoy the outdoors at home.

Enabling adults to enable children

When adults are comfortable and at home in the outdoors they become enthusiastic and attentive co-learners with the children. A supportive leadership team builds confidence, competence and self-belief, enabling practitioners to articulate the philosophy and practices of Natural Play. Staff feel good about themselves, consulted and truly part of the team and are eager to learn about and reflect upon the children and their play outside.

Putting this guiding principle into practice

Make sure **every adult has good clothing** and knows how to dress for the weather, so that they are always physically comfortable outside.

Provide many opportunities for **exploring outdoor activities for themselves,** such as water play and making a den, informally discussing the feelings and learning possibilities.

Find out what staff are not happy with or do not like about your current outdoor environment or provision – and **work on solutions together**.

At every individual supervision session and group staff meeting ensure that practice outdoors is discussed, so as to **give the support individuals need** to increase both confidence and competence.

GATEWAYS to natural play – the HOW of playing and learning outdoors

The Shared Vision and Values for Outdoor Play and Learning in the Early years is presented in the foundational Opening Up the Outdoors booklet, **Valuing the Outdoors** (White & Edwards 2018), cornerstone of the 'establishing beliefs' **WHY** strand (available from Muddy Faces).

GATEWAY booklets are produced through collaboration between Early Childhood Outdoors and Muddy Faces, to support the aims of the **Opening Up The Outdoors** initiative through the 'creating rich experiences' **HOW** strand.

Each of the **GATEWAY** booklets has a clear 'gateway' in provision and experience outdoors that it seeks to open. Each booklet offers a simple, straightforward and easy to implement aspect of development and action, which actually opens up much more of the outdoors than at first meets the eye. Further booklets will address keystone provision such as playing with the rain, loose parts, woodwork and tools, den play and storytelling.

Opening each gate initiates a great way of harnessing the outdoors for enjoyable and worthwhile exploration and play – contributing to opening up the full richness of playing and learning outdoors, and capturing the best the outdoors can provide for supporting all children to thrive and grow. For ongoing information about Gateway booklets as they become available, visit the **Outdoor Hub** at www.muddyfaces.co.uk